Norse Mythology
Gods, Myths, and Religion

© **Copyright 2020 by Creek Ridge Publishing - All rights reserved.**

This document is geared towards providing exact and reliable information in regard to the topic and issue covered. The publication is sold with the idea that the publisher is not required to render accounting, officially permitted, or otherwise, qualified services. If advice is necessary, legal or professional, a practiced individual in the profession should be ordered.

From a Declaration of Principles which was accepted and approved equally by a Committee of the American Bar Association and a Committee of Publishers and Associations.

In no way is it legal to reproduce, duplicate, or transmit any part of this document in either electronic means or in printed format. Recording of this publication is strictly prohibited and any storage of this document is not allowed unless with written permission from the publisher. All rights reserved.

The information provided herein is stated to be truthful and consistent, in that any liability, in terms of inattention or otherwise, by any usage or abuse of any policies, processes, or directions contained within is the solitary and utter responsibility of the recipient reader. Under no circumstances will any legal responsibility or blame be held against the publisher for any reparation, damages, or monetary loss due to the information herein, either directly or indirectly.

Respective authors own all copyrights not held by the publisher.

The information herein is offered for informational purposes solely, and is universal as so. The presentation of the information is without contract or any type of guarantee assurance.

The trademarks that are used are without any consent, and the publication of the trademark is without permission or backing by the trademark owner. All trademarks and brands within this book are for clarifying purposes only and are the owned by the owners themselves, not affiliated with this document.

Table of Contents

Introduction 1

Chapter I: History and Sources 5
    A Brief History of the Norse People 5
    The Mythological Accounts and Sources 10

Chapter II: Important Deities 15
    Odin 17

Chapter III: Mythology 25
    The Basics 26
    Norse Cosmogony 29

Chapter IV: The Nine Realms 34

Chapter V: Races and Entities 44
    The Divine Tribes 44

Chapter VI: Baldur's and Loki's Fate 51
    Baldur's Death 51
    Aftermath and the Binding of Loki 54

Chapter VII: Ragnarok 58
    The Story... 59

**Chapter VIII: Influence, Legacy, and
                    the Present Day** 64
    Impact on Scandinavian Cultures 65
    Cultural Impact beyond Scandinavia 66
    Norse Paganism Today 68

Conclusion...71

References 73

Introduction

In the centuries since the rise of Christianity and its adoption as the dominant religion and way of life throughout the West, many old folk traditions have been forgotten. To the uninitiated, it might seem like Christianity has been dominant in Europe since early in this millennium, but that's not necessarily true. In many Slavic nations, for instance, Christianity didn't take hold until at least the ninth century. In the wild and fairly isolated northern edges of Europe, the process of Christianization was a long one, lasting from around the 8th century to the 12th century. Some northern people, like the Sami, for example, didn't fully adopt Christianity until the 18th century.

The difficulties and the prolonged time required to Christianize these lands allowed earlier, pagan religions to survive much longer than in many other parts. The religion, mythology, and customs of the Norse people during that time were quite intricate and well-developed, which also contributed to their endurance. These North Germanic people held many beliefs, not just in their pantheon of gods but also about the world, cosmos, and reality as a whole.

Norse mythology has thus been studied for centuries, especially since the 17th century, after the emergence of additional important sources and materials. Among the pagan traditions the Christian faith replaced are some of the best-preserved records and descriptions of Norse religion and associated mythology. As such, we know a fair amount about how these people organized their societies and how they perceived the world.

Some concepts in Norse mythology speak of different worlds and realms of reality in ways that are quite foreign to Christian philosophy. However, some concepts aren't that distant to the Christian world, such as the idea of the first two human beings, Ask and Embla. This is just one of the many concepts and ideas that we know about in quite a bit of detail.

Traditionally, Norse people, particularly the Vikings, have been portrayed as little more than pagan barbarians and wildlings. While they are certainly famous for their raids against other European peoples, particularly in Britain, the truth is not that simple. Studies of their customs, social norms and mythology have revealed that these people were quite socially organized and definitely more than the savages that much of the world had known. In regard to shipbuilding and seafaring, for example, the Norsemen were at the very top of the game.

In this book, we will go over the many gods, myths, beliefs, customs, and traditions that make up the Norse mythology. As one of the most enduring pre-Christian European traditions, Norse mythology has had a profound impact on culture and folklore in Scandinavia and beyond, and, as such, it's important to learn about. This influence is also evident by the mythology's persistence in popular culture to this day. As such, Norse mythology and tradition make up one of the most important building blocks in European identity and continuity, serving as a bridge into a bygone era when the world was much different than what we know today.

Chapter I:

History and Sources

Before we delve into the intricacies of Norse mythology, it's important first to discuss the basics of who the Norse people, or Norsemen, really were. Where did they come from? How do they relate to the popularly known Vikings as well as the Scandinavian people of today? Norsemen or Scandinavians, as they are generally known today, are actually some of the oldest peoples in Europe in its entire history of human habitation, genetically speaking. That's not to say that Norse culture has existed for tens of thousands of years, of course, but that there are noticeable genetic overlaps between them and these ancestors, who were among the first humans to migrate to Europe.

A Brief History of the Norse People

By the time when humans started to settle in Scandinavia, most other regions in Europe were already inhabited. Some of the first settlers in Scandinavia were the Stone Age people who started to move in as the ice receded with the end of the last Ice Age. Scandinavia being a very cold, northern region, this recession of the ice sheets occurred as recently as 11,700 years ago. This is generally taken as the time when humans first began to settle in Scandinavia, particularly in parts of Denmark and southern Sweden. The settlements first formed along the coastal regions because they provided flatlands that were suitable for farming.

Another aspect of this ancient Scandinavian history is the Sami people. These hunter-gathering folks have inhabited parts of present-day Sweden, Finland, Norway, and Russia for around 5,000 years. They exist as a distinct group to this day, numbering some 80,000 to 100,000 people in the world. They are at their most numerous as minority groups in Sweden, Norway, and Finland. In the present-day Kingdom of Norway, the Sami people are officially recognized as indigenous.

The Nordic Bronze Age, which lasted roughly between 1,700 and 500 BCE, was another important epoch. Although the people in these lands were still not building larger towns or villages, they did expand, particularly within present-day Sweden and also for the first time to Norway. Farming and fishing became more widespread and sophisticated and were complemented by hunting. The Bronze Age Scandinavians also began to export certain goods during this time while drastically improving their skills in metalwork. The Scandinavian Bronze Age was followed by the Iron Age, which lasted until around 800 CE, giving way to the Viking Age, the most famous part of Scandinavian pre-Christian history.

The Norse people have been traditionally known to others as Vikings. This is because those were the Norsemen that these other peoples interacted with. As such, Viking is a term originating from scholars in the English-speaking world, especially since the 19th century. The word was and still is used to refer to those Norsemen who ventured out as various seafarers during a time of Norse expansion, also known as the Viking Age, starting in the late 8th century. These seafarers included traders, settlers, but especially warriors and raiders, who were particularly infamous for their raids in the British Isles and other places. What all of this means is that the

Vikings were Norsemen, but only some Norsemen were Vikings.

The Vikings and the Norse people, in general, are ancestors to today's nations that form the group of people we refer to as Scandinavians. These include Norwegians, Swedes, Icelanders, Danes, and the people of the Faroe Islands. The presence of the Norse people in some of these regions was the result of the aforementioned expansion and exploration. At the same time, the historical Norse heartland consists primarily of parts of present-day Denmark, Norway, and Sweden, which is where they originated. During their expansions, Norsemen went well beyond this region and the aforementioned countries as well. Around 900 AD, the Old Norse language was present in many parts of Great Britain, Ireland, Russia, Ukraine, the Baltic, Germany, and the countries of Benelux.

Before the Viking Age, the Norse people lived a profoundly rural, albeit agricultural lifestyle. At this point, these people had almost no settlements that could be considered towns, and their communities were very limited. They provided for their basic needs via agriculture, hunting, and fishing, especially in coastal regions. Norse shipbuilding during this time was a far cry from what it would be during the Viking Age. This was because their early boats relied on little more than oars.

A major breakthrough in Norse shipbuilding came with the advent of sails during the 7th and 8th centuries. The Norsemen soon developed the famous Viking longships as well, which propelled their seafaring capabilities to new heights. The longship wasn't invented overnight, of course, and forms of this vessel have been archeologically attested as early as the 4th century BCE. The final and most successful form was developed between the 9th and 13th centuries, though.

It was breakthroughs and ingenious solutions such as these that made Vikings some of the best seafarers in their day, eventually allowing them not just to visit but also attempt to colonize North America. As you may or may not know, this high-point of Norse exploration came some 500 years before Columbus reached the Americas. Norse attempts to colonize and permanently settle on American soil were ultimately unsuccessful, but they were an incredible achievement at that time, nonetheless.

The Mythological Accounts and Sources

A frequent question on many people's minds is how exactly we know so much about Norse mythology, religion, and traditions. Given that the Norse people relied heavily on oral tradition and taking into account how some other pagan traditions in the world were all but erased after making contact with Christianity, this is a fair question. Luckily, we actually have quite a few valuable sources, including poems, chronicles, inscriptions, and archeological evidence.

Many of these valuable writings are in Old Norse, with most of them originating in Iceland. Whereas Norse mythology and faith were largely passed on through oral tradition in other areas, the folks in Iceland made an effort to collect and record these oral traditions for the future. Particularly important were the writings that were put together in the 13th century, such as the Prose Edda and the Poetic Edda. The Poetic Edda is how we call an important collection of poems written by unknown authors in Old Norse. Much of this text originates from something called the Codex Regius, a medieval manuscript containing 31 poems. It is one of the most important sources that we have about Norse mythology. Not only are these writings important as a source of information, but they've also been a major influence on Scandinavian literature for centuries.

The Prose Edda, on the other hand, was written by Snorri Sturluson, a distinguished historian, poet, and politician in Iceland during the 12th and 13th centuries. Written in the early 13th century, the Prose Edda is most likely a combination of Sturluson's original works and pre-existing bits of writing that he had compiled. Just like the other Edda, the Prose Edda is an invaluable source of what we know about many myths of the North Germanic peoples, in general.

Apart from giving detailed accounts of various Norse gods and other things, the Prose Edda also provides a sort of manual on how skaldic poetry should be written. In simple terms, this is a traditional form of Old Norse poetry that used to be composed by skalds (poets). This poetry is characterized by the use of kennings, a type of alternate verses. Many of the writings that can be found in this Edda were contributed by skalds, who lived and worked before and after Christianity came to Norse lands. Another characteristic of the Prose Edda is its euhemerization, which means that the descriptions of the gods and other mythological beings portray them as largely historical, albeit exaggerated.

These are only two major sources that we have. Additional sources can be found among the Norse sagas, an enormous source consisting of thousands of written stories that have been kept in Old Norse. These tales speak of mythology and tradition but also chronicle the histories of some families in Iceland and other historical narratives.

Other important Norse sources include various runestones, which feature runic inscriptions about various topics. Runic inscriptions are simply writings written in the runic alphabet, which is an indigenous writing system used by ancient Germanic peoples far and wide. A particularly famous example is the Rok Runestone, which was inscribed around 800 CE and is now considered the first work of written literature in Sweden. Yet another runic source is the Kvinneby amulet, which dates to the 11th century and mentions the god Thor, among other things.

There are many other important writings but also objects that archeologists have uncovered over the years, all of which have helped us put together a clearer picture of what the Norse people believed. These bits of archeological evidence often include amulets that the Norsemen were buried with, which usually depict various subjects from Norse mythology, especially gods. Apart from written records and archeological evidence, old names of various locations have also helped us shed light on Norse mythology, particularly in regard to their gods.

All in all, records pertaining to Norse mythology are sometimes a bit scarce, and they are perhaps not as detailed and common as we'd like them to be, but they are still very valuable and useful. These pre-Christian traditions and myths are undoubtedly among the best-preserved and understood in the world. This is certainly owed in large part to the records, but the strength of Norse oral traditions is also crucial. On top of that, the fact that

Christianization throughout Scandinavia came later than in most of Europe and was a relatively slow process has also helped preserve important records that might have been lost or destroyed a few centuries earlier.

Chapter II:

Important Deities

There were many deities in the Norse pantheon of gods, but some of them are far better known than others. You're going to learn more about how these gods fit into the Norse beliefs and mythology as we go along, but first, we are going to take a bit of time to mention a few of the most famous and revered Norse gods. Many of the Norse gods were highly anthropomorphic and human-like, especially in regard to their relationships among themselves. The stories of these gods often read like history, although the deities are described as having many divine and supernatural abilities and influences.

Thor

Thor is certainly one of the most famous of the Norse gods, in great part owing to popular culture and media. Like many of the gods and myths we'll mention, Thor was featured prominently throughout the history and traditions of Germanic peoples far and wide, not just among Norsemen. Because of his importance, records give us quite a few valuable details about Thor as he was seen by the pagans who believed in him. Traditions around Thor were recorded as early as the times of Roman conquests in Germanic lands. Thor reached the height of his popularity during the Viking Age, though.

Thor is well known for his mighty hammer called Mjolnir and for his association with thunder and storms. He was also associated with trees, woods, strength, fertility, and he was also viewed as the protector of humanity. In many stories, Thor is also given a physical description, having red hair and beard as well as a powerful gaze. Thor's importance is best illustrated by his presence in many of the mythological tales and narratives, in which he plays prominent roles. Like other Norse gods, Thor has an intricate set of relationships with various other deities.

This mighty god is married to Sif, an earth goddess described in the Poetic Edda and the Prose Edda. Thor is also said to have had a relationship with the giant Jarnsaxa. Thor is also a father to numerous children, such as the goddess Thrud, whom he had with Sif and Magni, whom he had with Jarnsaxa. Thor has many other relationships with stepchildren, siblings, servants, and others. Still, his most famous feature is undoubtedly his Mjolnir, a hammer so mighty and heavy it can crush mountains. Numerous other aspects of Thor's appearance have been detailed, such as his Megingjord belt and his Jarngreipr iron gloves. Thor is also often described as owning a staff by the name of Gridarvolr.

Odin

Odin is another crucial deity in Norse mythology and a central figure in many mythical tales. Throughout the records of the narratives and the worship of Odin, there are many associations connected to him. Odin has been tied to wisdom, royalty, magic, frenzy, war, death, healing, knowledge, victory, the runic alphabet, and much else. Odin is also married to Frigg, the goddess of marriage, fertility, and wisdom, and he rules Asgard, one of the Nine Realms.

According to the common description, Odin has only one eye, a long beard, and is usually armed with a mighty spear by the name of Gungnir. He also usually wears a cloak and a wide hat. In his service, Odin has the wolves Geri and Freki, as well as two ravens by the name of Huginn and Muninn. These companions, especially the ravens, are said to keep Odin informed about all the affairs of Midgard, one of the Nine Realms that is inhabited by mortal humans. Another one of Odin's companions, so to speak, is Sleipnir, a flying horse with eight legs. On the back of this horse, Odin can fly all across the sky but also into the underworld.

Like Thor, Odin is part of a family and has many important relationships, notably with his parents, Bestla and Borr, and his brothers, Vili and Ve. Odin is also Thor's father, whom he had with Jord, the divine personification of Earth. Odin is father to many other sons as well, among them Baldur, the god of light, who was also the son of Frigg. Odin is also often described as a curious god in a constant quest for knowledge, which often ventures out into the world in disguise. Odin is also described as a fan of wagers, which he frequently makes with

Frigg, betting on the outcome of undertakings by humans and other beings.

Loki

Loki is a trickster god, viewed as the god of mischief, who is another rather famous deity from the Norse pantheon. He has an intricate set of familial relationships that vary by source and is described as a father to many beings, including gods and all sorts of mythical creatures in various animal forms, such as the serpent Jormungandr and the wolf Fenrir.

A particularly interesting aspect of Loki is the plethora of relationships he has with other gods, which are often quite checkered. Being a god of mischief, Loki is no stranger to making enemies, but judging by the records we have, he possesses a sort of dual nature. As such, Loki is sometimes helpful and kind to other gods while, at other times, he can be outright malicious toward them.

Loki's trickster title isn't earned just by his ability to fool others through lies and other regular means. One of his greatest tricks is his capacity for shape-shifting, which allows him to trick others in a wide variety of ways. Across the different tales involving Loki, he is said to have taken the form of a salmon, a fly, a mare, and also an elderly woman, illustrating that he is also capable of gender shifts. We will go into more detail on Loki's trials and tribulations later, but one of his defining characteristics is his eventual conflict with the other gods and his imprisonment. Despite his occasional kindnesses, Loki has ultimately committed a terrible crime that has alienated him from other gods and brought severe punishments upon him.

Further complementing Loki's role as a trickster is his great charisma and high intelligence. Apart from changing his form and appearance dramatically, Loki is also capable of creating all sorts of decoys, manipulating fire, creating illusions, and even becoming invisible.

Freyja

Another important deity, Freyja, is the Norse goddess of love, sex, beauty, fertility, and gold, but also of war and death. She is also known as Freya, Freyia, and Freja and belongs to the Vanir. The Vanir can most aptly be described as a class, family, or group of gods that have to do with fertility, nature, magic, wisdom, and foresight. Other members of this family include Freyja's brother Freyr, her father Njordr, and others. The Vanir is one of two main groups of Norse gods, with the second being the Aesir, which is made up of Odin, Thor, Frigg, Baldr, and Tyr.

Some physical descriptions of Freyja include mentions of her beautiful necklace called Brisingamen ("flaming ornament"), which is stolen and kept by Loki for a while. Freyja is also often described as having a companion in the form of Hildisvini, the boar, and riding a chariot that is pulled by two cats. She also usually wears a cloak made of falcon feathers.

Freyja is also described as the ruler of Folkvangr, which is best described as a heavenly field where many fallen warriors are received after the death. These warriors form one half of the fallen, while the other half go to Odin's hall of the warriors, the famed Valhalla. This is just one of the aspects that made Freyja very important to the Norsemen, given their focus on warfare. Freyja is also married to the god Odr, who is described as an often-absent husband, which is a source of great unhappiness for Freyja. According to Norse mythology, when Freyja cries because of her husband, she cries tears of red gold.

Baldr and Others

Baldr, the god of light, also known as Baldur, is another very important deity in Norse mythology. One of the reasons he is so important is that he is killed because of Loki's trickery, an important Norse tale that we will explore a bit later. Baldr is also attested as the god of joy, purity, and the summer sun and is noted for being the son of Odin and Thor's brother. Baldr is also father to Forseti, who is generally viewed as the god of justice and reconciliation. The significance of Baldr's death in the Norse mythological narrative is immense, both as a tragedy to the Aesir family but also as an event that sets in motion other events leading up to Ragnarok, which is essentially the apocalypse in Norse mythology.

Freyr, also known simply as Frey, is the god of prosperity and is another important deity described as Freyja's twin brother. He is also associated with virility, good weather, and sunshine, among other things. Freyr also plays a very important role in the mythology that is more characteristic of Sweden, where he was traditionally believed to be the progenitor of the Swedish royal house.

Other important deities, some of which we've already briefly mentioned, include:

- Tyr, the god of law;
- Heimdallr, the god of foreknowledge;
- Njordr, the god of the sea;
- Frigg, the goddess of marriage and motherhood;
- Ymir, the father and ancestor of all the Jotnar ("giants," singular: Jotunn),

and numerous others. You will learn more about these gods and beings as we delve into some of the mythological stories. At least ten to fifteen deities can be viewed as major deities in Norse mythology. Still, the number of various supernatural beings and creatures that are important to the narratives is far greater. What's particularly impressive about the Norse pantheon is how detailed and intricate the familial and other relationships between the gods are. Indeed, the family trees of the aforementioned divine families are well-preserved and very detailed.

Chapter III:

Mythology

Norse mythology is, more or less, an amalgamation of stories and beliefs that were passed down through generations mostly via oral tradition. These stories speak of all sorts of things relevant to Norse life and culture, including mighty battles, wars, magic, gods, love, and all those other things that humans have always given importance to. These stories were a way for the Norse people to make sense of the world around them and the universe, in general, but they were also used to teach morals and valuable life lessons. Of course, Norse mythology has also always been the cornerstone of Norse religious practices. In this and the following chapters, we'll focus on some key elements and narratives from Norse mythology, including a number of important tales.

The Basics

As you can probably gather, much of Norse mythology revolves around gods and various other beings, often with a focus on their relationships, struggles, exploits, hardships, and other experiences. Norse giants, referred to as the Jotnar, are particularly important for the mythological narrative, and they interact with the gods in all sorts of ways all throughout the stories. Some of the Jotnar are friends, lovers, or relatives to the gods, but many are also enemies to gods and humans. This is why, for instance, the god Thor often comes into conflict with various Jotnar and slays many of them according to numerous stories.

The god Odin is another aspect of Norse mythology that almost always pops up in conversations. This is partly because he is in charge of Valhalla, where Valkyries carry one-half of all the fallen warriors after their death. Valhalla is undoubtedly among the most famous concepts in all of Norse mythology. However, Odin's importance in the mythological narrative is even greater because it is said that he was the god who gifted mankind with the runic alphabet. What's more, he did this through a personal sacrifice that entailed hanging himself on the Yggdrasill. This is the unfathomably enormous, cosmological tree that holds together and connects the Nine Realms and thus the universe. Being more-or-less the spine of the universe, the tree of Yggdrasill is a vital part of Norse mythology.

Indeed, cosmology is an important part of Norse mythology, and the Norsemen were undoubtedly very captivated by questions concerning the nature, origin, and purpose of life and the universe. We will go into more detail about the different realms in the next chapter, but the essence of this belief is that the tree of Yggdrasill is at the center of the universe and that it connects nine different realms or worlds, all inhabited by different entities, creatures, and beings, including humans, gods, and others. Apart from gods and the Jotnar giants, the Norsemen also believed in elves and dwarfs who occupy their own place in these realms.

The cosmological tree has three main roots. One of these roots is inhabited by the Norns, which are generally described as female entities in charge of human and the gods' destiny. Something else that's often referenced in many stories is travel between different realms, especially by gods and other supernatural entities, when they want to interact with humans in some way. There are also entities that live on the tree itself, such as Ratatoskr, who is a squirrel and a messenger of sorts. Another dweller of the tree is Vedrfolnir, the hawk.

Like most other mythologies and religions, Norse mythology focuses on the matter of the afterlife a great deal. So far, we've mentioned two scenarios for warriors who can either be carried by Valkyries to Valhalla or end up in Freyja's Folkvangr field. A third realm where the dead might go is Hel, a dark realm of the dead ruled by Hel. There are other places where people can go after they die, depending on the location and other circumstances of their death. Sailors who die at sea, for instance, are usually taken by the goddess Ran, whereas those who die as virgins will go to the goddess Gefjon. According to some writings, the deceased not only dwell in these realms of the afterlife, but, in some cases, they can also be reincarnated.

The mythological narrative adhered to by the Norsemen focuses on the creation of the world, the trials and tribulations of all creatures, including gods, and finally, a cataclysm and rebirth. Of course, humans are a prominent part of that whole story, with many great heroes throughout the stories, such as King Gylfi and King Geirroth.

The final narrative surrounding the cataclysmic Ragnarok is one of the most important aspects of Norse mythology. It is also one of the best-preserved, most detailed mythological accounts that we have. This isn't just because the story was well-preserved but also because of the detail that the Norsemen themselves had put into the story. It is a very sophisticated and thorough take on an apocalyptic event, which is something that many civilizations have talked about in some form or another.

Norse Cosmogony

Like most mythologies and traditions in the world, Norse mythology and religion have striven to give answers to all those crucial questions that have been on human minds since time immemorial. Of course, one of the most important among these questions is how and why our world and the universe have come into being. Just like the Old Testament, Norse mythology offers its own "Genesis," so to speak, often referred to simply as Norse cosmogony. The account of Ragnarok, the Norse creation story is very detailed and thorough in its description of the events.

Somewhat similarly to the Book of Genesis, Norse mythology explains that there was nothing but the Ginnungagap at first. This was a deep abyss of total darkness, silence, and chaos. This chaotic emptiness was the thing separating the Muspelheim and the Niflheim, the homelands of elemental fire and ice, respectively. The Ginnungagap, however, was not strong enough to keep the two realms separate, and so the flames of Muspelheim and the frost from Niflheim slowly made their way to each other, chipping away at the darkness.

Once the elemental fire and ice finally met in Ginnungagap, the droplets from the melting ice created Ymir. Ymir, meaning "screamer," was the first giant and the ancestor of those who came later, as we mentioned earlier. Ymir is described as a destructive giant with an ability of asexual reproduction, making him a hermaphrodite. All Ymir had to do was sleep, and new giants emerged from his legs and were spawned from the drops of sweat from his armpits.

Other things were created by the melting ice as well until a cow by the name of Audhumla, meaning "Abundance of Humming" or simply a "hornless cow rich in milk," emerged. She helped nourish Ymir to even greater strength and nourished herself by licking the salty bits of the elemental ice. Over a couple-day period, this licking eventually shrunk the ice and revealed Buri, the god who was the progenitor and first ancestor of the Aesir gods. Buri's son, Bor, later married Bestla, the daughter of a giant, and they gave birth to Odin and his brothers.

As the story goes, Odin and his brothers would later kill Ymir and build much of the world from his parts. And so, the oceans were made of Ymir's blood, plants from his hair, earth from his skin and muscle tissue, and the sky and clouds from his skull and brain, respectively. Furthermore, the sky, or Ymir's skull, was held up by four dwarves. After the world was created, the gods made Ask and Embla, the first man and woman, from tree trunks. They were also provided with a secure home, Midgard, where they could be safe from hostile giants.

For many years, various experts from different fields have been putting great effort into analyzing and interpreting these myths. They tell us much about how the Norsemen and other Germanic peoples viewed the world, life, universe, and their own position therein. The symbolism and the depth of these tales also testify as to the sophistication of this culture that was once considered completely primitive and savage.

Ymir, the empty and dark Ginnungagap, and the creation of the universe can all be interpreted in numerous ways, and these elements contain various themes that can be found in other mythologies all over the world. Ymir himself can be viewed as personifying the chaos of the formless, void world before creation. One of the ways in which experts have interpreted these elements is that they symbolize potential that is yet to be realized. Just like in the bible, the darkness and the void before creation are empty and formless – it is nothing – yet at the same time, it contains everything the gods need to create the world.

Another important thing we can gather from this creation myth is that the culture that produced it was one that not only experienced but completely embraced conflict. In a warrior culture and society, conflict is usually seen as a way of life but also as a way of creation, so to speak, and Norse mythology is no different. As you can see, the very birth of Ymir was the result of a figurative clash between the elemental forces of ice and fire. The world itself is created from parts of Ymir's torn corpse. This tells us that conflict can be a creative process but also emphasizes the importance of sacrifice. This worldview is far from unique in medieval Norse culture, but their take on it was illustrated with great artistry and philosophical savvy.

Chapter IV:

The Nine Realms

The realm that we inhabit and perceive as humans is only one of nine connected and kept together by the great tree Yggdrasil. All of the beings in the universe, whether spiritual, physical, mortal, or immortal, have their place somewhere in these nine realms. Together, these realms form the core of Norse cosmology, and they provide a fairly detailed account of how the Norse people viewed the universe. While Norse writings refer to the Nine Worlds numerous times, they don't necessarily list all of them by name. The list of these realms is something that scholars have later compiled during their studies of Old Norse texts.

Asgard

Asgard, meaning "Enclosure of the Aesir," is described as a world or realm that resembles an enormous fortress and is home to the Aesir divine family. From the human standpoint and spirituality,

Asgard is located in the sky while also being connected to Midgard, the human realm. The link that connects the two is a bridge called Bifrost, which is essentially a great rainbow that leads up from earth to Asgard.

Numerous important locations are said to be within Asgard. Apart from the rainbow bridge of Bifrost, there is also Bilskirnir, which is said to be Thor's great hall. Freyja's Folkvangr field and Odin's Valhalla are both located in Asgard as well, which means that all fallen warriors will end up in Asgard. Odin also has his throne, called Hidskjalf, in this realm. This throne is important because when Odin sits on it, he is able to observe all of the Nine Realms. While Norse mythology has no concept of heaven, at least in the Christian sense, Asgard might be viewed as the closets equivalent.

Midgard

Midgard, translated as "Middle Enclosure," is the realm of mortals and, as such, great importance is ascribed to it all across pre-Christian Germanic traditions. One thing to note, Midgard and Asgard, is the underlying concept that's hinted at in the very names of these realms. The suffix -gard refers to the old Germanic dichotomy between innangard and utangard. Innangard translates as "inside the fence" and denotes all that which is in order, abides the law, and is civilized. Utangard, which means "beyond the fence," refers to the opposite, meaning chaotic, wild, and beyond the law.

The concepts of innangard and utangard don't refer exclusively to spatial locations but also to abstract things like human thoughts. What all this means is that Midgard is roughly somewhere between these two extremes. Asgard, on the other hand, is completely innangard. As such, it's often portrayed as something for humans to aspire toward, although it is unquestionably divine and beyond human reach. As far as humans are concerned, Midgard is also the only fully visible realm.

Joutenheim

The utangard realm that's the opposite of Asgard, according to the aforementioned dichotomy, would be Joutenheim, the "Homeland of the Giants." This uninhabited, chaotic realm essentially surrounds Midgard and is the place where giants dwell and roam, many of them hostile and destructive. The fact that Joutenheim surrounds Midgard is another reason for the human realm's name. In accordance with the utangard-innangard concept, the Joutenheim realm is also called Utgard.

Descriptions of what Joutenheim and its locales look like are numerous. Across the various accounts, this realm includes deep, dark forests, harsh and lifeless expanses, unforgiving and freezing mountain peaks, et cetera. It is an inhospitable place where no human could survive, on top of being invisible to humans. Important locations within Joutenheim include Mimir's Well of Wisdom, Thrymheim, which is the home of the giant Thiazi, the Vimur River, and other places. Many of these locations are mentioned in numerous tales detailing the quests and adventures of the gods. Often, the gods have to venture through the dangerous and unforgiving land of the giants to accomplish some goal.

Alfheim

Alfheim, meaning the "Homeland of the Elves," is where elves dwell. In old Germanic traditions, elves are not quite like gods, so they are viewed more as demigods and are a distinct race and class in Norse mythology. We don't have many descriptions of what Alfheim is like, as this realm is usually just mentioned in the writings without much detail. As well as not knowing what the realm looks like, we also don't know much about the relationship between the Elves and the gods. This is further complicated by the fact that Alfheim is said to be ruled by Freyr of the Vanir divine tribe. One description of the elves themselves notes that they are "more beautiful than the sun."

There are two significant mentions of this realm in Old Norse writings. One thing we can gather from the sources is that the rule of Alfheim was given to Freyr as a present when he was still a small child. Another mention of Alfheim describes it as the dwelling of the Light Elves, making a distinction between them and the Dark Elves who live in the earth.

Muspelheim

Muspelheim, which means the "World of Muspell," is a world inhabited by fire giants and sometimes just referred to as the realm of fire. As we mentioned earlier, it's one of the two realms separated by the abyss of Ginnungagap and plays a vital role in the creation of the universe. The fire giants who live in Muspelheim are also referred to as the sons of Muspell and are ruled by Surtur.

The meaning and interpretation of the word Muspelheim have been very important in the attempts of various experts to decipher details about the realm. References to "Muspell" are also found in Old Saxon and Old High German records, testifying to the age of the concept. In the oldest contexts that have been uncovered, the word most likely means something like "the end of the world through fire." In Norse writings, however, the meaning seems to revolve around a giant who leads his followers in a battle against the gods during the cataclysmic Ragnarok.

Niflheim

Niflheim is known as the World of Fog and is described as the home of mist, cold, darkness, and ice, as we mentioned earlier. This realm is located "north" of Muspelheim and is generally seen as its opposite, both as a location and as a concept. Niflheim is said to be ruled by Hel, the goddess of death, who is Loki's daughter and is described as half-life and half-rotting.

Some references describe Niflheim as the realm of the "dishonored dead," which means all those who die a cowardly death. That is usually taken to include most deaths that don't occur in battle. Apart from its important role in the creation and the birth of Ymir, Niflheim serves to illustrate further the importance the Norsemen gave to battle and warfare.

Nidavellir and Svartalfheim

It hasn't been determined beyond all doubt whether Nidavellir and Svartalfheim are one and the same or two separate realms. The confusion arises from the problems associated with the sources attesting these terms. A poem called The Prophecy of the Seeress, which is the older source is the first piece of literature that references "Nidavellir." On the other hand, Svartalfheim is mentioned in Snorri's Prose Edda, which is the only place where such mention can be found.

Even the mention of Nidavellir in The Prophecy of the Seeress is minor and doesn't tell us much except that Nidavellir is to the "north" and that it contains the "golden hall of Sindri's family." Because the Norse people often used the words "north" and "downward" interchangeably, we are able to assume that Nidavellir is underground. Furthermore, Sindri is a dwarf known from other Old Norse writings. Because his family's hall is golden, it's a solid assumption that he was an expert craftsman and blacksmith since this was a lucrative profession in the world of the Vikings.

At any rate, Nidavellir is generally taken to mean "Low Fields" or "Dark Fields" while Svartalfheim translates as the "Homeland of Black Elves." This is the realm of dwarves, essentially, and they are described as living underground in a world of many mines and forges where the dwarves work tirelessly at what they do best – blacksmithing and crafting. Snorri Sturluson is the only writer who refers to dwarves as black elves, and his writings on this subject have been the source of significant confusion, which is why it's still uncertain if these are two different realms. It's uncertain how much of this confusion resulted from Snorri's Christian influence, but it has ultimately led to confusion and misunderstandings regarding the world of the dwarves.

Vanaheim

Vanaheim is to the Vanir tribe what Asgard is to the Aesir – a home and base. This world can be considered as more in line with what we would consider "natural." One reason for that is the association that many of the Vanir gods have with things like fertility. Despite that possibility, Vanaheim was most likely imagined as an utangard world according to the chaos-order dichotomy we mentioned earlier. This assumption is based on its name, of course, and its "heim" suffix that it shares with other chaotic realms. Still, that doesn't mean that Vanaheim was imagined as a place in decay but that it was simply wild, as opposed to Asgard and Midgard, which are much more in line with the human concepts of order and civilization.

The location of Vanaheim in relation to the other realms is also uncertain. Some experts have also claimed that this realm was another mythological element invented by Snorri Sturluson, but this is unlikely because mentions of Vanaheim were found in original, Old Norse poems.

Chapter V:

Races and Entities

Norse mythology is filled with all sorts of supernatural creatures that humans share this universe with, as you can see. They all have their roles to play across the realms that they inhabit. You will learn a few more things about these entities as we explore additional myths. Still, in this chapter, we'll go over details about some races and entities that we've already mentioned and touch upon some that we haven't.

The Divine Tribes

You already know what the Aesir and Vanir divine tribes or families are and which gods belong to them. However, there's a fair bit more to the story, including various interactions between these tribes and the lore that accompanies it. What separates this Norse concept from other similar ideas, such as the Titans and the Olympians in Greek mythology, is that these two families are generally seen as equals in strength, importance, and other ways.

One important event that's referenced numerous times is the Aesir-Vanir war. What we know about this legendary struggle comes from fragments. Still, it was more likely a war of unification that was largely inconclusive but eventually led to the unification of the two families. It's also written that during this war, like on other occasions, the two divine families exchanged hostages.

Elves

Elves are another distinct race of entities that we already mentioned, and it's one of the particularly popular elements of Norse mythology in the modern era. This is evident by the fact that elves have made their way into all sorts of fantasy literature, films, cartoons, and other media.

In Norse and other Germanic religions, these beautiful creatures enjoy a very high status and are connected to both divine tribes, although they themselves are only demigods. One of the defining characteristics of elves is an ambivalent attitude and relationship with mankind. For instance, elves are recorded as making people ill while, at the same time, having powers that can heal them, which they often do in exchange for sacrifices. Norse mythology also suggests that humans and elves can produce offspring.

Dwarves

It might come as some surprise, but dwarves in Norse mythology are never described as short and feisty men with thick beards. These ideas and interpretations came later. In Norse mythology, dwarves are invisible entities mentioned in many old Germanic traditions.

The one thing that Old Norse writings tell us about the exact appearance of dwarves is that they are completely black creatures that dwell under the ground in their Nidavellir realm. It's also said that dwarves will turn into stone if touched by sunlight. Being such gifted blacksmiths and craftsmen, the dwarves were the ones who created many of the weapons and other legendary items mentioned throughout Norse mythology, such as Thor's hammer. Other things said to be built by dwarves include Odin's spear, Freyr's ship, Freya's necklace, and much else.

Giants

As you now know, giants play a very prominent role in much of Norse mythology. In Norse religion and other Germanic traditions, giants are generally treated as a tribe of their own. In fact, there isn't much indication that they were viewed as anything less than the gods, especially not in power or importance. While more-or-less equal in those respects, giants are still very different than the Aesir and the Vanir. Gods and giants are thus seen as opposing forces that are still connected in many ways. After all, the gods created the universe by using Ymir's body.

Similarly to the dwarves, the true nature of these "giants" has been somewhat lost or altered in translation. The word we use implies something colossal, but that's not necessarily how the Norse people viewed the Jotnar. There is a long linguistic history behind how the word giant came to be used here, but the fact is that the Proto-Germanic words from which the Norse names for the "giants" came would perhaps be better translated as "devourer" and "powerful and injurious one."

More so than concerning themselves with the size of these entities that were believed to be beyond human reach and sight, the pre-Christian Norse people focused on other concepts that we have already mentioned. Above all, the "devourers" were destructive entities and forces that lived "beyond the fence" (utangard). While the gods of the Aesir are generally seen as the creators and patrons of the realms of order and of civilization as humans see it, the "giants" are the opposite. They are the forces that dwell somewhere out there and are constantly threatening to harm and destroy the world that humans know and understand.

Norns

The Norns, which we've only briefly mentioned as creatures living at one of the three main roots of the Yggdrasil, are female entities who are important because of their sway over fate. The Norns are sometimes mistakenly treated as an afterthought by observes simply because so much of Norse mythology revolves around the gods and their exploits and adventures. The Norns, however, are technically much more powerful than the gods and were thus feared by the Norse people.

The Norns are described as being very numerous and having their origins among other races, mostly gods, elves, and dwarves. This is just one less common view, though. Based on other writings, notably the Prophecy of the Seeress, the Norns don't come from any other races and are their own breed. According to this view, there are only three of them, and they are named Urdr ("The Past"), Verdandi ("What Is Presently Coming into Being"), and Skuld ("What Shall Be"). These three Norns are said to control time and all that happens in it.

Valkyries

The Valkyries are another mythological race of creatures that's quite famous in the popular culture of today. These "Choosers of the Fallen" are simply the spirits who help Odin, especially with collecting his half of fallen human warriors, which he needs for his army when Ragnarok comes.

The most popular view on what the Valkyries were like describes them as elegant and beautiful women who carry fallen warriors to Valhalla with great care. This interpretation was popular during later times in Viking history and especially among collectors and writers who dealt with Norse mythology after Christianization. In the earlier days, however, the Valkyries weren't all that pleasant. In fact, they were fairly scary and more malicious. It was believed that they chose only the best among the fallen warriors and that they even decided who would get killed in combat. As such, the Valkyries commanded a fair amount of fear. To make matters worse, once the Valkyries would choose a warrior, they would use all sorts of "evil" magic to ensure that he would fall.

Chapter VI:

Baldur's and Loki's Fate

As we already mentioned, an important part of the Norse mythological narrative is the death of Baldur and the string of repercussions resulting from this woeful incident. As the son of Odin and Frigg, Baldur was greatly revered and respected among the gods. He wasn't beloved just because of his lineage, though, as Baldur is described as a brave and generous character who was full of joy, which he brought with him everywhere he went.

Baldur's Death

The events surrounding Baldur's death began when he started to have dreams that were foreshadowing a dark fate in the near future. This dream was taken as a message and a warning not just by Baldur but also by the other gods who became deeply concerned for Baldur's wellbeing. As such, Odin took it upon himself to discover the meaning of the dreams that his son was having.

On this quest, Odin mounted his horse, Sleipnir, and rode all the way to the underworld to seek answers from a seeress who ended up there when she died. She was remembered as a seeress with an extraordinary ability to decipher dreams, so Odin knew he had to go to her. Before he arrived, Odin assumed one of his disguises in which he often traveled throughout the realms. Once he was there, Odin noticed that the halls of the underworld were adorned and prepared for a great feast. The seeress explained that the coming feast was prepared as a festivity of welcome for Baldur. She was implying that he was about to die, before she realized that she was talking to a disguised Odin.

Upon learning these saddening news, Odin could do little more than return to Asgard and inform the other gods, all of whom loved Baldur dearly. Frigg was especially shaken by the impending death of her beloved son, and so she went on a quest around the universe, pleading to every entity, creature, and thing not to hurt Baldur. She managed to get all the things in the universe to make an oath not to do any harm to Baldur, and the gods of Asgard were relieved. As a way of celebrating, the gods started playing a game where they threw sticks, rocks, and other things at Baldur, having a laugh at his new-found invulnerability.

It was at this point that Loki, the trickster god, decided to make his malicious move, as was in his nature. He asked Frigg if she had really managed to get every single thing in the cosmos to pledge not to harm Baldur, to which she said that the only thing that didn't swear an oath was the mistletoe. As she explained, the mistletoe was so harmless that she felt no need to ask. Loki then went to the mistletoe and made a spear from it, which he then brought back to the other gods.

Among these gods was Hodr, a blind god, who was thus vulnerable to Loki's trickery. Loki took advantage of the fact that Hodr was being left out from the game due to his blindness, and he offered to give him a branch to throw at Baldur. The "branch" was the spear, of course, but Hodr had no way of differentiating a branch from the spear's shaft, so he threw it according to Loki's direction. The spear easily made its way through Baldur's body, and he fell dead where he stood.

The gods were horrified by this killing not just because Baldur was beloved but also because they all knew his death was the harbinger of the cataclysm of Ragnarok. After the initial shock, Frigg asked for one of the gods to go down to the underworld and make an offering to Hel as a way of ransoming Baldur back to their realm. One of Odin's sons, the god Hermod, volunteered for this task.

Aftermath and the Binding of Loki

The gods then held a grand funeral for Baldur with all the traditions taken into account. Baldur's pyre was made from his ship, Hringhorni, and the gods gathered to send the pyre out to sea. The ship wouldn't budge, however, and no matter how hard they tried, the gods couldn't force it out of the sand. They thus sought help from Hyrrokkin, a giant and the strongest entity in the universe. After being summoned, she arrived on her wolf that she reined with venomous snakes. Hyrrokkin was able to move the pyre but not before making the entire world shake. The sight of Baldur's body being brought onto the ship was so devastating that his wife, Nanna, fell dead in her grief. After the fire was lit, Baldur was finally sent on his way.

While this grand funeral was taking place, Hermod continued on his journey deep into the underworld. After riding for nine nights and having to answer to Modgud, the giantess on the river Gjoll, he finally entered Hel's realm. Once he entered Hel's throne room, he saw Hel on her throne and Baldur on a seat next to her. The following morning, Hermod presented his and the other gods' case to Hel, telling her that Baldur was the most beloved god in his realm and that the entire world weeps for him. Hel then presented Hermod with a seemingly simple condition. She said that if Hermod could get every single creature in the cosmos to weep for Baldur, she would let him go back to Asgard. If not, Baldur was going to remain with her forever.

With the help of other gods, Hermod was able to send messengers throughout the cosmos and get everyone to weep except the giantess Tokk. This giantess was, in fact, the disguised Loki, and his answer was simple: "Let Hel hold what she has." This sealed Baldur's fate as an eternal captive of Hel's, robbing the realms of the living of the joy and happiness that he had brought to all.

Loki already had a history of conflict with the other gods, of course, but his involvement in the death and subsequent condemnation of Baldur was the final straw. When Loki learned that the gods were out to capture and punish him, he fled to an isolated house on a high mountain peak. He spent his days holed up in this house and hiding in a river, disguised as a salmon. Loki did this when the gods were informed about the location of his hideout by the all-seeing Odin. The gods were onto him, though, and they quickly made a fishing net, and, after some difficulty, they managed to catch him. This was primarily thanks to Thor, who caught Loki by his tail fins as he tried to leap one last time toward the sea.

The gods gave no quarter to Loki, and their vengeance was merciless. They brought Loki to a cave along with two of his sons, one of whom they turned into a wolf. That brother was then set on the one who was still in human form, tearing him apart while Loki had to watch. The wolf ripped out his former brother's entrails, which the gods then turned into chains with which they tied Loki to three great rocks.

Loki never repented, and the gods inflicted an additional punishment by putting a venomous snake above him, from where its venom would drip directly on Loki's face. As the legends say, Loki's wife, Sigyn, was there to help him by holding a bowl over his head to catch the poison. The bowl, however, had a limited capacity, so Sigyn had to take it away to empty it periodically. Every time she did this, the poison would fall on Loki's face, making him shake and convulse in pain. This, in turn, is said to be the cause of earthquakes in Midgard, the realm of humans. Loki's punishment was to remain in this horrible state until the time of Ragnarok, when he was destined to break free from bondage and help the giants to destroy the universe.

Chapter VII:

Ragnarok

As we briefly mentioned throughout this book, Ragnarok is one of the most important aspects of Norse mythology and religion. It is a cataclysmic event that brings about the destruction of the entire cosmos and, as such, it is the disastrous closing chapter in the mythological narrative. For the Norsemen and Vikings who lived during a time when this set of beliefs was the established religion, Ragnarok was the apocalypse that was expected to come sometime in the future. Although it represents the ultimate destruction of everything, including humans and the gods, Ragnarok can also be viewed as a tumultuous rebirth of sorts.

In Old Norse, the word Ragnarok means "Fate of the Gods," but it has also been referred to as Ragnarokkr, which is more in line with "Twilight of the Gods." Apart from these names, some writings have also called it "Aldar Rok," which means "the fate of mankind." Because of its implications in regard to the fate of the entire universe, the concept of Ragnarok had a great influence on the Vikings and their lifestyle and traditions.

The Story

The tale of Ragnarok begins by stating that the Norns would decide the exact date it was all to happen. Whenever it is, it will start with Fimbulwinter, the "Great Winter," the likes of which have never been seen before on earth. This winter will last three times the length of a normal winter, and it will be far colder and much worse than all the winters before, even by Norse standards. The winds are described as horrifically cold and blowing from all directions, and the sun itself will falter. The cold that will ensue will lead to a complete collapse of all social systems, norms, and organizations. People will abandon their morals, and all constraints will be lifted as desperation sets in among the starving mankind. In the ensuing struggle for bare survival, even family members will kill each other.

Ragnarok will also have a profound impact on the course of many ongoing legends that the Norsemen believed in. One example is Skoll and Hati, the legendary duo of wolves that forever chase the sun and the moon, trying to eat them. When Ragnarok sets in, Skoll and Hati will finally catch up with their prey. It's also foretold that the stars will disappear from the night sky, and unyielding darkness will envelop the world. As the cosmological tree of Yggdrasil begins to tremble, all the trees and the mountains will fall and crumble.

Even the mighty and horrifying wolf Fenrir will break free from the chain with which he was bound, finally free to devour everything in his path. Another monstrosity that will rise is Jormungand, the Midgard Serpent. This sea monster dwells at the bottom of the ocean that surrounds the human realm and, when Ragnarok comes, he will leap out onto the land and spill all the seas.

Naglfar, the legendary and mighty ship made from the fingernails and toenails of the dead, will break free and sail across the flooded world. This ship and the army of giants that it will carry will all be under the command of Loki. The giants and all the other forces that will descend upon the tangible world of men during these days will represent the utangard chaos that finally crosses the "fence" and seeps into the world to destroy order.

Fenrir and Jormungand will wreak more havoc all across the world as Fenrir devours everything in his path, and Jormungand spits out a horrible venom on the land, sea, and in the air. Additional giants will make their way into the world from the fire realm of Muspelheim as a great crack opens up across the sky like a portal. Led by Surt, the fire giants will march on from Midgard, using the Bifrost rainbow bridge to cross into Asgard and finally slay the gods, as was foretold. Even though the gods are aware of the prophecies, they will decide to stand their ground and fight. The armies of gods and giants will clash on the field of Vigrid, the "The Plain of Surging Battle."

In this battle, Odin will lead his army of select warriors from Valhalla in an attempt to slay Fenrir. This is foretold as a charge more courageous than any before it in the history of all warfare. Nonetheless, Fenrir will devour Odin and his entire army. Enraged, Odin's son, Vidar, will charge at Fenrir and successfully avenge his father, finally slaying the beast.

After that, the god Tyr will clash with another of the great wolf beasts, Garm, and they will kill each other in the process. The same thing will happen between Heimdall and Loki as well as between Freyr and Surt, the leader of the fire giants. All the while, the mighty Thor will come to blows with Jormungand and successfully put an end to the monstrous serpent's reign of terror. By that time, however, Thor will have already been poisoned by Jormungand's venom, and he too will fall after taking nine steps.

In the aftermath of this terrible struggle, what remains of the earth will be swallowed by the depths of the ocean; the world will preside over a void, a nothingness. This conclusion is described as the complete and utter undoing of everything that had ever happened up until that point, including the creation of the universe and all the struggles and exploits of people, gods, giants, and other creatures inhabiting Yggdrasil's realms. That is according to one view, at least.

Another view holds that this is not the end but merely a rebirth and a new beginning. Slowly across time, a new and luscious world will start to take form, adorned with greenery and all manner of natural splendor. According to this version of events, Vidar, Vali, Baldur, Hodr, and two of Thor's sons (Modi and Magni) will have miraculously survived the apocalypse. Furthermore, one human couple will have also survived in hiding in the Wood of Hoddmimir. Their names are Lif and Lifthrasir, which translates roughly as "Life" and "Striving after Life" from Old Norse. Of course, this couple will repopulate the world and all its new lands under a new sun that is described as the daughter of the old one.

The ensuing age is said to be an era of prosperity and peace. The emphasis that some sources put on peace in this instance is quite interesting and perhaps hints at a certain longing for peace that always exists in the human heart, even in a society as warlike as the Vikings were. According to some poetry, however, a dark shadow slowly emerges on the horizon of this new, seemingly perfect world. That shadow is Nidhogg, the enormous, dark dragon that most interpretations equate with a warning that Ragnarok will return.

Chapter VIII:

Influence, Legacy, and the Present Day

As you are probably well aware, Norse mythology remains one of the most prominent pagan traditions in public discourse. Its influence has certainly been very notable for centuries, and nowadays, that influence is mostly reflected in the customs and traditions that Norse religion and mythology have helped shape in modern Scandinavian nations. Of course, the influence is also reflected in popular culture and media all over the world, especially in Europe and America.

Norse paganism is also still practiced in various forms by numerous religious organizations that work to keep the faith alive. These organizations are generally marginal, and their members are a tiny minority, of course, but they do a lot to keep the old traditions going. It's for these reasons that Norse mythology and religion can still undoubtedly be considered influential.

Impact on Scandinavian Cultures

From the very beginning, Norse mythology played a central role in determining the culture, way of life, philosophy, and priorities of Norse society. As we have already established, conflict was an integral part of the Norse worldview, and much of their philosophy and many of their values revolved around warfare, victory, and courageous death. Norse religion religious beliefs were a powerful source of motivation to go into combat and either win or die. As the Vikings saw it, the glory was theirs either way. Needless to say, this cultural attitude made the Vikings formidable warriors who were always eager and excited to get in a fight. This was undoubtedly a warrior culture, and the Norse religion was at the core.

At the same time, Norse mythology also illustrates a profound curiosity and sense of wonder that the Norse people cultivated. While their eagerness for war and their propensity to raid other lands made outsiders see them as little more than savages, the Norsemen were actually deeply fascinated by the world and the universe. They asked many questions, and the answers that they came up with show us that these were creative, curious, and philosophical people. In a way, this curiosity was what fueled their impressive explorations, which, as it turns out, were probably the most far-reaching and successful in the world during that time.

Of course, all of this had a profound effect on the direction this society developed in and all those spawned from it. The societies in Scandinavian countries nowadays are completely different, of course, as Christianity and other post-pagan factors have shaped it. Still, there is an undeniable historical continuity, and some influences have managed to slip through the cracks, like elsewhere in the world. These things are reflected in small cultural phenomena and menial customs, but they are not very pronounced. More than anything else, Old Norse mythology and the Viking Age, especially, are important as integral components of identity and heritage in the Scandinavian nations.

Cultural Impact beyond Scandinavia

The influence of Norse traditions, especially culture, went far beyond Scandinavia. While it's true that Christianity ultimately won and was adopted as the religion and way of life throughout Scandinavia, it would be a mistake to think that this influence only went one way. The Vikings exerted great influence on all the peoples that they came into contact with and conflict with, and this influence manifested itself in all sorts of ways, including architecture, art, language, cuisine, military tactics, and much more.

The most tangible cultural influence of the Vikings and Norse mythology today is certainly to be found in popular culture and art. This influence mostly began with the reimagining of sorts that happened to the Vikings during the 20th century. For a long time, the Vikings were viewed as nothing but reasonless savages by many, but during the 20th century, they gradually became noble savages. Even though neither of these ideas is really true, as you know now, the change in perception did spawn a lot of renewed interest.

This is how we got so many works of art and pieces of media about Vikings, some idealizing them, some trying to portray them objectively, and some running wild with the stories. From comics over music (mostly metal) to the epics of fantasy like Lord of the Rings, the influence and fascination that Norse mythology causes can sometimes appear endless in contemporary society. A more recent phenomenon, of course, is video games, among which there are many titles, both fantastical and historical, which draw great inspiration from Norse mythology. Interest has been rekindled even more in recent years thanks to projects like the History Channel's Vikings historical TV series. Perhaps interest will wane over the next few decades, and, in the future, this era of renewed interest will appear as a mere blip in popularity, but for now, the fascination by Norse mythology all over the developed world seems stronger than ever.

Norse Paganism Today

Once Christianity took over the last parts of Scandinavia and became the dominant faith, the preceding Norse religion and traditions didn't just vanish overnight, of course. People continued their way of worship and their customs in secret, and some even did it subtly through Christian rites. Some folks continue to practice the Norse religion to this very day, although there is no longer any real danger of being severely punished for doing so. In Scandinavia, the practice survives with numerous customs and rituals such as outdoor gathering, the making of offerings to the gods, et cetera. The problem with reviving this religion has always been the lack of records. While we know much about the mythology itself, our knowledge as to the practical side of Norse worship is limited. As such, modern Norse paganism is mostly a reinterpretation more than an exact imitation.

Nowadays, religion exists most prominently as Heathenry. It's known by other names as well, such as Heathenism, Germanic Neopaganism, et cetera. This revival, which is generally classified as a new religious movement, first gained prominence and started to develop during the 20th century. Communities exist mainly in Denmark, Iceland, Sweden, Norway, and some in the US and UK. One of the more common names for this religion in Scandinavia is Asatru, which is a term coming from Iceland and meaning "Aesir belief."

In Denmark, though, the main Norse religious organization is called Forn Sidr and is the only one officially recognized and approved after it was founded in 1997. Its name ("the old way") comes from the way in which the Norse people referred to their old traditions once they came into contact with Christianity, which was "the new way." Forn Sidr has around 600 members today, while it's believed that only around 20,000 people practice Heathenry in the world at large. As such, it's certainly a marginal religious community, although it has an upward trend in some places. In Iceland, there are around 3,000 members, and Asatru is among the fastest-growing religions there.

Conclusion

The things you've just learned about Norse mythology and religion have probably cleared up a few things about contemporary popular culture as well, on top of teaching you about the topic itself. This further illustrates the historical importance and value of these enduring myths and traditions. For a long time, Norsemen were viewed as little more than pagan savages in the face of expanding Christian influence. The clash of these great cultures went on for a long time, and it produced a rather interesting fusion of culture and identity.

In the time that has passed since the heyday of Christianization in Europe, we have learned that the pre-Christian Norse people weren't as simple as we once thought. Their societies were complex, and their system of beliefs was well-developed. On top of that, they really excelled at the things they focused on, such as shipbuilding and seafaring.

All in all, Norse mythology and religion has given us a window into a world that could have easily been lost to time. The spread of our contemporary Abrahamic religions has facilitated the disappearance of many pre-existing faiths and traditions over the centuries. Traces of these faiths were also sometimes purposely erased, which means that we will never know about many myths and religions that might have existed in the corners of the world that, for a long time, were untouched by Christian or Islamic civilizations.

Mankind's seemingly innate need to believe and to try to explain the universe and its mysteries has produced intricate philosophies and mythologies wherever humans reached. The study of these old faiths and philosophies is important to our own understanding of pressing questions concerning values, morals, faith, and much else. Norse mythology and religion form one of the best-preserved examples of such a philosophy and are certainly an invaluable piece of world heritage.

References

https://www.ancient.eu/Vikings/

https://www.ancient.eu/Norse_Mythology/

https://www.ancient.eu/article/1305/nine-realms-of-norse-cosmology/

https://mythology.wikia.org/wiki/Norse_mythology

https://en.natmus.dk/historical-knowledge/denmark/prehistoric-period-until-1050-ad/the-viking-age/religion-magic-death-and-rituals/the-old-nordic-religion-today/

https://www.livescience.com/32087-viking-history-facts-myths.html

https://www.historyextra.com/period/viking/vikings-history-facts/

https://libguides.csi.edu/c.php?g=676302&p=6634177

https://www.lifeinnorway.net/scandinavia-before-the-vikings

https://norse-mythology.org/tales/

http://www.sourcinginnovation.com/archaeology/Arch07.htm

https://ancientnordicreligion.weebly.com/nordic-influence-in-society.html

Milton Keynes UK
Ingram Content Group UK Ltd.
UKHW020859210224
438192UK00006B/72